BUYER
&
SELLER
BEWARE!

REAL ESTATE QUESTIONS

YOU NEED TO KNOW

AS A SELLER AND AS A BUYER

BY: JUAN F. HERNANDEZ V

(BUYER & SELLER BEWARE!)
Copyright © 2015 by (Juan F. Hernandez V)

ISBN-13: 978-1503009998
ISBN-10: 1503009998

Dedication

I would like to dedicate this book, to the United Property Owners Association. I could not have written this book without the members of this group. Read it and share it with your family and friends.

Table of Contents

Disclaimer ....Page 6

Introduction ....Page 7

Chapter 1

WHAT DOES THIS BOOK DO FOR YOU? AND WHO IS IT FOR?

Page 10

Chapter 2

HOW IS THIS BOOK STRUCTURED? AND WHY?

Page 23

Chapter 3

QUESTIONS TO ASK A SELLER OF A SINGLE-FAMILY HOME

Page 33

Chapter 4

QUESTIONS TO ASK A SELLER OF RAW LAND AND VACANT LOTS

Page 50

Chapter 5

QUESTIONS TO ASK A SELLER OF MULTI-FAMILY DWELLINGS

Page 67

Chapter 6

QUESTIONS FOR THE SELLERS TO THE BUYERS

Page 83

Chapter 7

FINAL THOUGHTS

Page 93

Motivational Quotes………………………………... 96

Must Read Books…………………………….....… 97

Contact Info…………………………………….…… 99

DISCLAIMER

This book was written with the standpoint of real estate regulations that are or were in the State of Texas, where the author practices. Other state laws and federal laws may vary since the publishing of this book. However, the overall information in the book should be helpful in obtaining information for a seller and buyer of real estate in the State of Texas.

No legal, estate, financial, business, or tax related advice is given or implied. The opinions expressed in this book are the author's and are based on his experiences working in the Texas real estate market. The reader with information regarding real estate investing in general and the author's investing strategy in particular.

The reader should be aware that real estate laws and practices vary from state to state, and, of course, are subject to change. While the information provided in this book is believed by the author to be true and accurate, the author takes no responsibility for any unintentional mistakes or omissions.

The reader is advised that this book is intended as a general guide to real estate investing, not as legal or professional advice pertaining to individual situations. The author disclaims any liability that may result from the application of the information relayed in this book.

Introduction

I would like to start off by saying if I can write this book than anyone can write and publish a book. I have no university education; (no Degree), and not because it wasn't around or the opportunity was not there but because I choose to be stubborn and not want to listen or pay attention during high school or college.

When I was in high school I became very interested in real estate. I was 16 years old when I got my first job working for my father's property management company. He had me in charge of answering phone calls and taking messages in the property management office. Which may seem very easy to some but when you are 16 years old and still in high school, the performance of your job isn't always on your mind. Instead I started thinking of other distractions and hanging out with the wrong friends that kept me from my goals and dreams. I made many mistakes during that time. Some of my mistakes were no brainers. I was just not paying enough attention to detail (reading between the lines).

I replaced those distractions with something called *"Me Time"*. *"Me Time is the time you and only you are around"*. During this *"Me Time"* I would think of all kinds of inventions or ideas of just random things and I would write them in this notebook I had stashed away. I still remember when I started writing in my 1st notebook. I would right positive messages to myself, I would write goals, ideas, my thoughts, my wants, my needs, and work towards everything I wanted in my life. It was a complete rush to me I wanted to get things done fast and right. I soon learned that if I wanted to advance fast I must know myself and know how I learn.

Once I began gathering information about myself I studied and studied it. I realized I like things to be very simple and straight to the point.

Every time I would read a new book or study a new subject. It seemed to never be something I really wanted to do. Most of the time it was because of the time it took to read a book. Some books were 200 pages others were 500 pages. I hope to have come up with a simple easy to read a book that is under 200 pages but can give you great guidance to gathering the right information for many different types of real estate deals.

I think list are easy and straight to the point. Throughout my life, I developed several notebooks of lists of basically whatever it is I wanted or needed. Lists have changed my life and hope they will change yours as well. This book will go on to discuss and show lists of questions that will help your real estate transaction be successful. Happy Reading.

CHAPTER 1

WHAT DOES THIS BOOK DO FOR YOU? AND WHO IS THIS BOOK FOR?

First of all I want to thank you for taking interest in my book. I made this book to help expand knowledge and creative thinking to the reader of this book. One of my deepest passions is to spread the wealth of my real estate knowledge to everyone I know. I really enjoy helping people understand what questions to ask when looking at a piece of real estate. Giving someone a simple formula or a list I came up with and seeing how the list or formula changes their business plan, is what I enjoy doing. I get a real kick out of it! This book was made to explain and help anyone understand how I analyze a piece of real estate.

This book was also made for people that are thinking of getting into real estate investing, and also people who are already in real estate from full time investors to the high school students just finding out about real estate this book will help you. I know if I had the information that is in this book when I got started in real estate that a lot more of my deals would have went way smoother than they did.

When I began writing this book there were 2 main reasons that stuck with me the whole way thru the writing of this book. The number one question I got all the time was who is this book for? Well, it's for you! When I say you, I mean the reader of this book who took the time and interest in expanding their minds. How you came across this book is a mystery in itself. Maybe I sent it to you because I thought this book would help you. Maybe you purchased this book because it was an easy read and affordable. Maybe you are looking for an extra source of income in real estate. Maybe you just want to learn something new when talking to sellers and buyers of real estate. Well this is the book for you no matter what reason. We all need a place to live so learning the information in this book will be very helpful when looking for your next home, land, or multi-family dwelling.

Second question that I asked myself was, what does this book do for the reader? This book is to help you when making phone calls, emails, or having a face to face conversation with a seller and a buyer of real estate. Let's say you are driving down the street in your neighborhood when you see a sign in the yard of a beautiful piece of Real Estate (Home, Land, or Apartment Build). You might even see the property online and you may say to yourself, I'm going to call them and see what the seller is asking. So you call them up and you get an asking price! Now what? Well next is knowing what it is you're looking at and understanding what questions to ask yourself and the seller.

Understanding what a piece of real estate is; is very important. There are valid and invalid pieces of real estate. Real estate to me is only valid when the property has a recordable deed with a title policy and/or a title commitment. If the deed is not recordable you will run into problems most of the time. If you do not have a recent or new title policy, this will be another problem.

Back to what real estate is, real estate can be confusing to most. Most think a piece of land, a small or a large home, it can also be an apartment complex, condo, or townhome, mall, warehouse, and the list goes on and on about what real estate is. The true and correct answer about what real estate really is; real estate is everything under and above (bundle of rights) your land or "dirt" is considered real estate and the houses and buildings are improvements to the real estate.

I have learned that gathering the right information when you are interested in buying or selling real estate is very important. In fact gathering information is the most important factor in real estate because with bad information you have bad results.

A deed is a recordable document that proves ownership of real estate in Texas. That is as simple as I can put it. I have learned thru experience, that a deed should be filed and recorded in the county clerk's office. Each county has one filing and recording office (Easy to find online). If the real estate is being purchased with financing; a general warranty deed with a vendor's lien is filed and recorded along with a deed of trust, the promissory note does not have to be filed in Texas. Again these are recordable documents and are practiced in Texas. Check your local laws before exercising anything in this book. A promissory note is also involved in a financing transaction. Usually the note is held by the lender but, sometimes the lender sells the promissory note to a 3rd party. The promissory note is negotiable, always remember that.

A title search, title commitment, and title policy are usually handled thru a title or escrow company, which charge a fee. Always remember that you should not buy a piece a real estate without going thru a title company. This will usually be taken out on the seller's side of the settlement statement. I say usually but in recent times it is common to see in contract offers that the buyer pays closing cost due to a seller's market in Texas. Title searches can also be done at the county clerk's office or online for a fee as well. The title search will give you the previous deeds that have been recorded. I usually only will get a separate title search if I'm looking to purchase real estate at a sheriffs sale or tax assessor sale.

Remember when I said make sure you have a recorded deed? Well if your deed is not recorded then the deed does not appear on the title search. If that ever happens, which it happens a lot to say the least. You will have major problems getting a new title policy and possibly losing your property. The title search will show most of the liens if not all of the recorded liens on the property.

The way I do business is not the same for everyone. I will not and do not purchase real estate without a deed that is recordable and that I can record myself. I usually get a general warranty deed sometime with a vendor's lien if I'm financing the property. In Texas where I practice real estate, when financing a property you will get a deed of trust and a promissory note (which the note is negotiable) along with a general warranty deed with a vendor's lien. I have, under certain circumstances received what is called a special warranty deed. A special warranty deed is only insured by the title policy for the time of ownership by the previous owner of the property (Foreclosures, estate sales, etc. are typically special warranty deeds). Buyers beware of special warranty deeds; always do your own research. I always get a title search, and/or a title policy on every piece of real estate I purchase. No matter what! (Title policy comes with a title search and title commitment)

One of my favorite parts of any real estate transactions is the negotiating time. Negotiating is one of the most heard of things or verbs that gets thrown around like it's easy. Negotiating is an art/skill. I would say more of an art that takes years of practice and studying.

Negotiating starts as soon as you make a phone call, email, or communication about a property and ends at the closing table (hopefully). I say hopefully because I have run into a few deals that have had some misrepresentation issues and required more negotiating even after we closed and funded the deal. Everything is negotiable even after the deal is closed and funded. So for me it's very important to know which questions to ask the seller, broker, agent etc. I also found it very important to know how much time to spend on each question and how to ask the question itself.

Many big time investors will not sit down and talk to an inexperienced person for more than 2-5 minutes. Make sure you know what you are talking about. Many big time investors will not give you the little information that will help you become very successful at obtaining information. This book is going to give detailed questions that the pros of real estate use to obtain information when inquiring about a piece of property.

Let me say this, THIS BOOK is not just for beginners! I say that because this book is made up of many of my own trials and errors. This book also contains lists of many of my friends which are fellow investors themselves, family, and other people's real estate transactions and stories, I've heard in my years as a real estate investor.

In the pages to come you will learn the questions I came up with while I was working for my father's property management company until now as a full time successful real estate investor. The questions are in a how-to format. The questions will cover a buyer's and a seller's position on real estate transactions, such as:

➢ Land

➢ Single-family homes

➢ Apartment Buildings or Apartment Houses

This Book is also going to help you, if you want to sell your own home using a licensed broker or agent, or if you don't want to use a real estate broker or agent when selling your property on your own. It will also save you time and headaches by helping you screen the *"tire-kickers"*.

Let's face it we all want the best price for our property when we sell it. I can't say this book will get you the highest price for your home. I can say it this book will help you screen the buyer in a more effective way to get you the right buyer for the property you are selling. Finding the right buyer has its own challenges itself. I hope to make the process a little bit easier for you.

This book is mostly from a buyer's point of view. I get asked all the time how do I get started in real estate when I have no credit, money, or time. I usually tell that person to read more if they disagree with me, then I tell them that they simply are not cut out for real estate. Many people are in fact cut out for real estate and could become very successful but choose not to read or study documents. Real estate is all about reading and reading thru the lines of BS.

This book will help you, if applied correctly; meaning if you are not ready with a pen and paper when making your phone calls then this book is not going to help as much. You must be aware and be prepared while using this book. Have your pens and paper close by you at all times. If your plan is to become a full time investor in real estate then you better have your tools (pens and paper) ready. Keep reading more informative books to get a better understanding of what you are doing and want to do in real estate.

In the next chapter to come, I will break down the reason of why this book is structured the way it is. I really hope you understand how important it is to write things down!

CHAPTER 2

HOW IS THIS BOOK STRUCTURED?
And WHY?

I structured this book for the average reader who doesn't want to read a 300 to 500 page book on real estate. Basically this book is going to be short and simple. This book will help you get the information needed in order to make a better decision for the time and the money you invest in real estate transactions. I structured this book a certain way to make it very easy to read and understand for anyone 15 years old and older. My father use to tell me, if a young teenager in high school can understand it, anyone can.

During the time I worked in my father's property management company. I had started to make lists of questions to ask both the sellers and the buyers of real estate properties. He would send me to buy office supplies, tools, and building material to take to the properties. I would get chances to drive around a little and look for signs in the yards of potential properties I could maybe buy, well

I thought, I could buy anyway; while dropping off supplies to different apartment complexes.

The kind of driving around I did was a bit different than most. I would go block by block, street by street in different neighborhoods I thought I could or wanted to buy in. I would make my rounds I called it, about once or twice every week. I found a lot and a lot of signs in yards of land, single-family houses, as well as multi-family dwellings, once I really started to pay attention.

I would write down the phone numbers from the signs and write down the addresses of the properties I was interested in. I would get lucky some times and see the seller outside, I then would park the car and get out and talk to the seller, or I would call and sometimes have to do some investigating research if the building was either boarded up or fenced in.

I look at various different types of properties still to this day. I get interested in certain properties I just don't understand so I like to look, not buy at bad deals. Not to make a bad choice or get tricked into buying, but to see how or why the deal became bad so I do not make the same mistake as the seller.

Another reason is to expand my mind to what else is out there. You may have a better opportunity or better luck than the last investor, buyer, or seller had, but you have to read the market before doing anything. I have a rule. If I do not understand the deal in 5 minutes, I simply stop and go study more about that subject I do not understand and then go back to the deal. If the deal sells to another buyer then that's what happens, it's not worth getting upset about.

You have to be aware there are sharks out there! Before you purchase anything in real estate, Get It In Writing! Study it ahead of time. You might say to yourself, where can I get to study a deed, a title policy, a mortgage. I will tell you if you do not know it's called the internet. I have seen it time and time again certain people who choose not to study contracts and paperwork are the ones that do not succeed or enjoy real estate.

I choose to study and it paid off. I've made mistakes just like everyone else such as:

a) Not knowing what to say when I would call the phone numbers I had collected while making my rounds, losing potential deals is how I looked at it. I fixed that by creating notebooks and lists which I'm converting into books like this one.

b) Losing or misplacing the information after I had wrote it on a napkin or small piece of paper. I fixed that by carrying a notebook with 3 pens in the glove box.

c) Another mistake I made was not having a pen, or paper to write down the phone numbers and addresses of the signs I would see. I fixed that by carrying 3 pens in the glove of my car, 5-6 pens next to each phone in the house with a notebook, and I would carry 1 or 2 pens in my pockets with a pocket notebook.

Those are all no brainers now, but back then it was a habit I had to develop. Once I developed the habit of keeping pens and plenty of paper to write down information. The process of obtaining information on real estate for the purpose of someday owning real estate was beginning to get easier and more interesting.

After I got my paper and pens together, I went at it calling and calling different sellers and buyers of real estate. The information I was obtaining, a lot of the information I did not totally understand. Especially when it came to multi-family dwellings, but not understanding something is part of the process of learning.

During my spare-time (goal time) I would research on the internet, what I did not understand during the process of obtaining the information. Slowly but surely I was learning more and more. The more phone calls I made the better I became at making the correct choice of analyzing the property to be a good or bad deal, all because

I became aware and got prepared to develop my skills through a list.

Making lists and talking notes about your own personal mistakes and flaws helps you become driven and your mind begins to develop this inner goal-setter that flies out on to the paper. I have yet to see a self-made anything or self-made anyone, who have not written down their goals, flaws about their personal character, and so on. Writing down your own life and organizing it is part of the process of becoming successful at anything you choose to do, you must become organized with your thoughts and ideas.

In order for me to write this book I had to get my thoughts and ideas on paper. I have so many ideas for all kinds of subjects so I had to make my lists and take my time to understand what it is I wanted to do. I realized by writing in my notebooks I could go back and review my thoughts of what I was thinking about last week to 9 years ago when I got started in real estate. I began to see big changes in my thinking patterns when it came to real estate.

I would spend 4-5 hours per day, reading books, studying videos on the internet, going to real estate network meetings, etc. I realized that real estate was my choice, my destiny; I just enjoy owning real estate and I also enjoy learning on new ways to acquire and protect real estate.

Most of the books and videos I studied were sometimes too advanced or just plain old boring subjects. In order to become successful I knew I had to study more so in the back of my mind while sitting in some boring seminars. I would remember what I had been telling myself, if you want to be rich this is what you have to do. I would drill that phrase into my head every day. It seemed as if every day I was running into a challenge that I didn't want to do but knew I must do it in order to get to my ultimate goal.

Along the way I would meet some really nice and helpful people. They would ask me questions about why I enjoyed real estate so much. How can I get started with no money? I would invite them to lunch or dinner. I would explain my reasons for starting in real estate and my passion to continue real estate.

I would listen to their wants to get started but I would not see the action of reading and networking. Every last one of them would say they were too busy or couldn't or didn't want to. They just wanted to know how to make money and get it overnight, that was it. I would make relationships with people because we were either in the same business or they had a role in mine. I would try to spend more time explaining the reasons to read and write. The more time I spend the more time I felt was wasted on my end. That changed when I wrote this book. It helped me give my friends and fellow investors the shortest get to the point book.

I realized I could still help without wasting my time. I was no longer telling them to read a 300 to 500 page book. I was telling them to look at my lists. I decide to type them out and make 200 pages or less books to help anyone interested in real estate get information at a faster rate.

Didn't take long, before I knew it I was taking everyone out to lunch a lot of the time the other people I invited would pay for my meal. I have a vast amount of knowledge of real estate for someone my age, I kept hearing.

So I took it to the next step or level and wrote a book. This is my first book so please don't judge if the grammar or spelling is off a little. I never give up and I never will.

Follow these steps and you will and can do anything! Now check out these lists from real estate pros I've studied under. I promise you will learn something!

CHAPTER 3

<u>QUESTIONS TO ASK A SELLER OF A SINGLE-FAMILY HOME</u>

The questions in this chapter are organized to be in sequence of one another. This is by no means the standard way of asking questions but it sure helps as one of the best references I've ever came across in my years of real estate. This list of questions is by no means the correct way or wrong way to ask about real estate properties. It's just a good outline or guide to have and to share with friends and family for the purpose of getting a better understanding of what questions need to be asked or what information needs to be obtain in order to make a decision in buying a piece of real estate.

Some if not most of the questions are going to be questions the seller or the buyer may not want to answer. Be aware and be prepared to do some of your own research. By doing your own research you can save a lot of these questions and only ask the main questions you need in order to do your research. So read carefully and try to understand the creativity of the questions and the information in this book.

INFORMATION ABOUT YOURSELF

- What types of properties are you interested in purchasing?
- Do you want a large house or a small house?
- What do you plan on doing with the house fix & flip or hold & rent?
- What kind of financing do I have lined up to purchase this house? (Cash, Conventional financing, Private money, Hard money, Etc.)
- Do you want a large a lot of acres or do you want a small city lot?
- What sort of amenities do you want?
- Is this purchase going to be my last purchase?
- Are you an owner/operator?

NOTE: You must find this information out while you are obtaining information. If you can answer most of the questions in this 1st section then you will be able to use this book to its full power.

1) <u>GETTING INFORMATION ABOUT THE SELLER</u>

- What is your name and good contact information to contact you back (make sure you get a phone number, fax number and an email address)?
- Do you need to sell or want to sell your house?
- How soon do you need to sell?
- What do you have for sale?
- What is the reason you are selling your house?
- How long have you been trying to sell your house?
- What did you pay for the house?

- Have property values gone up since you purchased the property and by how much?

- How many other homes in the neighborhood are similar?

- Is this a short sale?

- Has the lender agreed to short sale the property?

- Is there a copy of the agreement or disagreement I can review?

- How many short sales have the bank approved in the last 6 months?

- Are there any foreclosures in the area?

- Is the reason you're selling your home due to a foreclosure or short sale in the area?

- Was the house to suit you and your family or was the house resold to you?

- Are you working a real estate broker or agent?

- Are you listed on the MLS (multi-listing service)?

- If not, ask them why they do not have a real estate broker/agent?

- Can I help you selling your house?

- Will you compensate me, if I find you a buyer for your house?

- Do you know of any other home owners in the area selling or that have sold their houses?

- If so, do you know if your home is competitive to the market/surrounding area?

- Will you consider seller financing the house?

- If so, what sort of down payment would you consider?

- How much per month would be suitable for you to sell?

- How much are you asking?

- Do you have comparable sales for the last 6 months?

- Do you have any written offers?

- Do you have any other properties for sale?

- If so maybe we can work out some sort of deal, where I can purchase all of them?

- Do you know anyone else selling a house?

- Do you buy and sell homes full time or frequently?

- When was the last time you bought or sold a home?

- How long have you lived in the area?

- Are you from the area the home is in?

2) <u>GETTING GENERAL INFORMATION ABOUT THE HOME</u>

- What is the address of the property?

- When can I come see the property?

- How long have your owned the property?

- Is the house free and clear?

- What kind of neighborhood is it?

- Are there any inconveniences? (Traffic, long entry, Noisy children)

- How close is the freeway? (Noise level, Access factor)

- What are some of good places to shop in the area?

- How are the schools in the area?

- Are there any HOA fees? (Home Owner Association)

- How many bedrooms are in the house?

- How many bathrooms are in the house?

- What is the square footage of the house?

- What is the square footage of the land or lot the house is on?

- How much are you asking for your home?

- Are you flexible on the price at all?

- Are you will to help with the closing cost?

- How much do you need to clear or net on the sale of your home?

- What do you like or enjoy the most about your house?

- Does the home have any special features?

- Do you have any manuals or paperwork for the special features?

- Has the house ever been in a flood?

- Are you in a flood zone?

- Do you have a flood insurance policy?

- Do you have a wind storm policy?

- Have there been any deaths on the property or in the house?

- Have you gotten the home inspected recently or in the past?

- When was the last time insulation was placed in the walls and in the attic?

- How old is the paint and sheetrock?

- What warranty do the A/c units have?

- Have the appliances been replaced or updated?

- Do any warranties come with the appliances?

- Have the appliances been repaired recently?

NOTE: When a home is built next to the coast line, in most cases roofs, windows, and others things such as drainage must be engineered and certified.

3) GETTING DEED AND TITLE INFORMATION ABOUT THE HOUSE

- Is the home in your name or in a company entity?
- Do you have a clear title on the property as far as you know?
- Do you have a general warranty deed on the property?
- How soon can you produce a clear title policy?
- If I can pay all your closing cost will you consider a lower sales price?

NOTE: If seller has a special warranty deed, quit-clams deed or anything other than a general warranty deed seek more research or ask if he has any addition paper work.

- Which title company was used in the previous closing of the property?

- Ask the seller if they have any of the previous closing paperwork such as :

  - Title commitment

  - Deed

  - Escrow Agent

  - Attorney

  - Settlement statement or Closing statement

NOTE: You will be surprised how many homeowners have their closing papers in their possession but choose to misplace them. Or choose not to share that information with you. I never understood why someone would misplace the papers that have to do with the roof over their heads.

4) <u>FINDING OUT ABOUT LIENS, PROPERTY TAXES, AND LAWSUITS</u>

- Are there any back taxes that are owed on the property?
- If yes, how many years of property taxes are delinquent?
- Ask them, if they have the total amount of delinquent property taxes that are due?
- Do they have a payment plan set up with the county?
- Do they have any receipts of any payments towards the property taxes?
- Are the current year of property taxes paid?

- Are you currently in any type of lawsuit with this property?

- Has this property ever been in any type of lawsuit?

- If so, what was the outcome of that lawsuit?

- If a judgment is the response, what kind of judgment does the property have?

- Are there any liens, judgments, or mortgages on the property that you are aware of?

- If yes, what type of liens, specifically?

- How did you get a lien on your property?

- How much are the liens?

- Do you owe a mortgage on your house?

- If so, what kind of mortgage do you have?

- How much do you still owe on the mortgage?

- What is the interest rate? And is it a fixed or variable rate?

- How many years are left on the mortgage?

- Are there any pre-payment penalties?

- Is the mortgage assumable?

5) <u>GETTING INFORMATION ABOUT THE</u>
   <u>CONDITION OF THE HOUSE</u>

- In your opinion what is the overall condition of the house?
- Any recent updates done to the house? (Such as: kitchen cabinets, counter-tops, bathrooms, etc.)
- If you had an extra 10 to 15 thousand dollars, what would you update or fix in or out of your house.
- Is the property on public water and public sewer system or well and septic?
- If on well and septic, ask when the well pump was last replaced or repaired?
- How is the well pump wired up to get electricity?
- How deep is the water well?
- Is the water well regulated by the state?

- What type of septic system do you have?

- Also ask if the septic is full or has had any recent repairs?

- How old is the roof on the house?

- What kind of roof is on the house?

- What kind of foundation is the house on?

- Is the foundation level?

- Has the foundation been recently repaired?

- If so, do the repairs of the foundation have a transferable warranty?

- How about plumbing issues?

- Have you had problems with the shower, sinks, or toilets?

- How about electrical issues?

- When was the electrical panel last updated? And who was the installer?

- Do you happen to know anyone at the local permit department?

- Are there any red-tags from the local permit departments or from the fire marshal's office?

6) <u>WHAT IF THE HOUSE IS RENTED OUT TO A TENTANT?</u>

- Is the home currently vacant?
- Is the home currently being rented?
- How much is the rent amount?
- Is the rent amount you are charging competitive to the market area?
- Are any of the utilities or bills paid by the landlord?
- How long have the tenants been living in the house?
- Have they had any trouble paying rent?
- Do you currently have the house insured?
- How long is the lease?
- Is the lease in writing or an oral agreement?
- Are the tenants current on the rent and utilities?

- When the house was vacant, roughly how long did it take to make it ready for renting?

- What was done to the house to make it rentable?

- Any major repairs done to the house itself or was it just cleaning up and painting?

- Does the house have working a/c units?

- What kind of A/c units do you have?

- How old are the A/c units?

- When the A/c units were last repaired?

- Will you consider a lower price?

CHAPTER 4

<u>QUESTIONS TO ASK A SELLER OF RAW LAND AND VACANT LOTS</u>

1) GETTING INFORMATION ABOUT THE SELLER

- What is your name and good contact information to contact you back (make sure you get a phone number, fax number and an email address)?

- What do you have for sale?

- How did you acquire the land to begin with?

- Do you need to sell or want to sell your land?

- What is the reason you are selling your land?

- How long have you been trying to sell your land?

- How soon do you need to sell?

- Are you working with a real estate broker/agent?

- Are you listed on the MLS or any other multi-listing service companies?

- If not, ask them why they do not have a real estate broker/agent?

- Can I help you selling your land?

- Will you compensate me, if I find you a buyer for your land?

- Will you consider seller financing the land?

- If so, what sort of down payment would you consider?

- How much per month would be suitable for you to sell?

- Do you know of any other land owners in the area selling or any other land that has been sold?

- If so, do you know if your asking price is competitive to the market/surrounding area?

- Have you had any strong offers?

- If so why haven't you accepted?

- Do you have any other land for sale?

- If so maybe we can work out some sort of deal, where I can purchase all of the land?

- Do you know anyone else selling land?

- Do you buy and sell land full time or frequently?

- When was the last time you bought or sold some land?

2) GETTING GENERAL INFORMATION ABOUT THE LAND

- What is the address of the land?
- What is the legal description of the property?
- What county is the property located?
- When can I come see the land?
- How long have your owned the land?
- What is the square footage of the land?
- How much are you asking for your land?
- How much do you need to clear or net on the sale of your land?
- What do you like or enjoy the most about your land?
- Has the land ever been in a flooded?

- Are you in a flood zone?

- Are you in a flood way?

- Are you in a flood plain?

- Do you have a flood insurance policy?

- Do you know the elevation of the land?

- What was the property tax bill last year?

- Do you have any tax advantages on the property?

- What is the assessed value of the property from the tax records?

- Does the land have any deed restrictions?

- What is the land zoned as?

- Have you applied for any permits to build?

- How is the land accessible? Road, boat, or plane?

- What is the land used for now?

- How long has it been used as, (whatever it has been used for)?

- Can the land or lot be easily converted into a something of more value?

3) GETTING DEED AND TITLE INFORMATION

ABOUT THE LAND

- Is the land in your name or in a company entity?

- Who has to sign on the deed to sell the land?

- Do you have a general warranty deed on the land?

- Do you have a copy of the deed I can read and review?

- Do you have a clear title on the land as far as you know?

- How soon can you produce a clear title policy?

- If I can pay all your closing cost will you consider a lower sales price?

__NOTE__: If seller has a special warranty deed, quit-clams deed or anything other than a general warranty deed seek more research or ask if he has any addition paper work?

- Which title company was used in the previous closing of the property?

- Ask the seller if they have any of the previous closing paperwork such as :
- Title commitment
- Deed
- Escrow Agent
- Name of Attorney
- Settlement statement or Closing statements

4) FINDING OUT ABOUT LIENS, PROPERTY TAXES, AND LAWSUITS

- Do you have the property tax id number or parcel number?

- Are the property taxes currently paid in full?

- How much are the property taxes?

- Are there any tax benefits in this land?

- Is the property currently in a tax suit or foreclosure?

- Are there any back taxes that are owed on the land?

- If yes, how many years of property taxes are delinquent?

- Ask them, if they have the total amount of delinquent property taxes that are due?

- Do they have a payment plan set up with the county?

- Do they have any receipts of any payments towards the property taxes?

- Are the current year of property taxes paid?

- Are you currently in any type of lawsuit with this property?

- Has this property ever been in any type of lawsuit?

- If so, what was the outcome of that lawsuit?

- If a judgment is the response, what kind of judgment does the property have?

- Are there any liens, judgments, or mortgages on the property that you are aware of?

- If yes, what type of liens, specifically?

- How did you get a lien on your property?

- How much are the liens?

- Do you owe a mortgage on your land?

- If so, what kind of mortgage do you have?

- How much do you still owe on the mortgage?

- What is the interest rate? And is it a fixed or variable rate?

- How many years are left on the mortgage?

- Any pre-payment penalties?

- Does the property have any utilities, such as; water well, septic tanks, meter pole for the electricity, gas lines with meter, etc.?

- Are there any un-paid city fines or tickets for uncut grass or junk cars?

- Is there any un-paid permit fines?

- Is there any un-paid judgments or liens?

5) DEVELOPMENT OF THE LAND

- How can the land be developed?

- What is the price per square foot to build?

- How long have you been a developer?

- How long have you been in the business?

- How many homes do you build per year?

- Are you insured and bonded?

- Can you provide me with that policy information?

- Do you have any references?

- How long will I have to hold on to this land until the development trend comes to my area?

- Is there a temporary use for the land until I can sell it? (Trees farm, Mini storages, etc.)

- How long will the development take?

- How can this land or lot be divided up?

- How much money does it cost to maintain the land?

- Who maintains the land? (Who cuts the grass, fixing fences, and etc.?)

- What are the selling and listing rates of land per square footage?

- Is the land leveled?

- How does the property get water to it?

- How is the electricity connected to the property?

- Are there any nearby stores or restaurants to help the development succeed?

- If so what type of stores and restaurants are they, major brand places or mom and pops stores?

- What other types of vacant land or lots are in the area?

- Can the land be used as a parking lot?

- Are there any existing permits on the property?

- Is the property fenced?

- How much frontage do you have?

- How many entrances are there to the property?

- How much of the land is to be used for retention and detention?

- Are there any mineral rights on the land?

- If so what are they?

- Has the seller been approached to sell the mineral rights or minerals?

6) <u>QUESTIONS TO DEVELOPERS, BUILDERS, &</u>

   <u>CONTRACTORS</u>

- What is the amount of concrete you will use to pour this slab?

- What is the thickness of the slab?

- What is the thickness of the Re-Bar?

- What is the minimum and maximum span of Re-Bar?

- What is the thickness of the beams?

- What is the span of the beams?

- Will the slab need any piers?

- If so, how many piers will be needed?

- How deep will the piers be?

- Is the engineering of the slab included in the price?

- What company will you be using to engineer the slab?

- If I can find better quality materials at a cheaper price will you be able to reduce the price?

- What kind and size studs will you use? (2x4 studs are standard)

- Where do you buy your lumber and materials?

- How do you save on wasted lumber? (cuts)

- What kind of decking do you use on the roof?

- What do you use on the overhang of the roof?

- Which shingles do you use for the roof?

- What sort of ventilation is used for the attic?

- What will the roof line look like when completed? (facial board or no facial board)

- Do gutters come installed?

- How many lights are on the exterior and where will they be?

- What kind of windows will be used?

- Will you use z-mold flashing or any flashing around the windows?

- Will the installer warranty the windows?

- What kind of interior and exterior doors will be used?

- What is the amp-age to the house? (120 amps, 150 amps, 200 amps, etc.)

- What brand of breakers will be used?

- What kind of wiring will be used for plugs and switches? (12-2 wire)

- How many lights are in the kitchen and bathrooms and where are they located?

- What sizes are the restrooms?

- What size is the shower or tub?

- What kind and size of toilets will be used?

- What brand of shower fixtures and faucet fixtures will be used?

- Are the faucet fixtures brass or plastic?

- Are parts easy to located and affordable for the light fixtures, toilets, faucets, and shower fixtures, etc.)

- How deep is the kitchen sink?

- What thickness are the sinks?

- What kind of pipes are you going to be using for sewerage, water supply, water heater, etc.?

- What thickness is the sheetrock?

- What kind of corners will be used? (plastic or metal)

- What kind of wood are the cabinets made out of?

- Will the drawers and inside of the cabinets be finished?

- What kind of countertops will be used?

- What kind of carpet and padding will be used?

- What is the thickness of the carpet and padding?

- If vinyl is used, what is the thickness of the vinyl?

- If hardwood is used, what is the thickness of the hardwood and what kind of wood?

NOTE: If building on pier and beam you will want to know the follow questions.

- What will you be using for piers? (Concrete blocks, telephone post, railroad crossties, etc.)

- What will you be using for beams? (4x6 is the standard)

- What kind of floor joists will you use?

- What is the span on the floor joists?

- How much crawl space will be under the house?

And the list continues with you and your inputs please send me an email with any suggestions.

CHAPTER 5

<u>QUESTIONS TO ASK A SELLER OF MULTI-FAMILY DWELLINGS</u>

1) <u>GETTING INFORMATION ABOUT THE SELLER</u>

- What is your name and good contact information to contact you back (make sure you get a phone number, fax number and an email address)?

- What do you have for sale?

- How did you acquire the property to begin with?

- How long have you been trying to sell your property?

- Do you need to sell or want to sell your multi-family dwelling?

- How soon do you need to sell?

- Are you working with a real estate broker/agent?

- Are you listed on the MLS or any other multi-listing service companies?

- Have you had any strong offers?

- If so why haven't you accepted?

- If no strong offers have been presented ask why not?

- If not, ask them why they do not have a real estate broker/agent?

- Can I help you selling your multi-family dwelling?

- Will you compensate me, if I find you a buyer for your property?

- Do you have any other properties for sale?

- If so maybe we can work out some sort of deal, where I can purchase all of the properties you have?

- Do you know of any other multi-family dwellings in the area selling or any others that have sold recently?

- If so, do you know if your asking price is competitive to the market/surrounding area?

- What is the reason you are selling your multi-family dwelling?

- Will you consider seller financing the property?

- If so, what sort of down payment would you consider?

- How much per month would be suitable for you to sell?

- Do you know anyone else selling multi-family dwellings?

- Do you buy and sell Multi-family dwellings full time or frequently?

- When was the last time you bought or sold some multi-family dwellings?

2) <u>GETTING GENERAL INFORMATION ABOUT THE DWELLING OR DWELLINGS</u>

- What is the address of the property?

- How long have your owned the property?

- Do you have a profit and lost statement?

- If so, ask if you can see it as soon as possible?

NOTE: If not you will have to ask a lot more questions

see section: 2-5 of this   chapter

- When can I come see the property?

- What is the square footage of the dwelling or dwellings?

- What is the rentable square footage?

- What is the square footage of the lot or land the dwelling sits on?

- How much are you asking for your property?

- How much is that per unit?

- What is the price per square foot?

- How much do you need to clear or net on the sale of your property?

- What do you like or enjoy the most about your property?

- What were your insurance costs last year?

- What is the property insured for? (Amount and Coverage)

- Does the property require windstorm insurance?

- How much is the windstorm insurance policy per year?

- Are you in a flood zone?

- Are you required to have flood insurance?

- Do you have a flood insurance policy?

- Has the property ever been in a flood?

- Does the property have any deed restrictions?

- How is the property accessible? Road, boat, or plane?

- What is the property used for now?

- How long has it been used as, (whatever it has been used for)?

- Can the property be easily converted into a something of more value?

- Does the property have a laundry facility?

- If so, do the machines come with the property or are they leased thru a 3rd party?

- If leased washer and dryers, how long is the lease and how much?

- What kind of tenant mix do you have? (blue-collar or white-collar tenants)

- What is the apartment unit mix?(how many 1 bedrooms, 2 bedrooms, and 3 bedrooms)

- What kind of leases do you have with the tenants? (Written or Oral leases) (Apartment Association Leases or Hand written)

- How long are the leases? (month-to-month, 6 months, or 1 year leases)

- What capital improvements were made in the last 24 months on the property?

- Do you have the information on who performed the work of the capital improvements?

- Do you have any un-paid debt with those contractors?

- Do you have any transferable warranties?

- Do you have any outstanding permit fees with the local city department?

- Do you have all the required certificates to operate your business?

- Is the certificate of occupancy transferable?

- When was the property last inspected by the local city department?

- If the property doesn't have a certificate of occupancy, find out what is lacking?

NOTE: You can go to the local city inspection department and request to get a copy of the inspection report.

3) GETTING DEED AND TITLE INFORMATION ABOUT THE DWELLING

- Is the property in your name or in a company entity?

- If the property is held in a company, what kind of company entity is the property held in?

- What kind of deed do you have?

- Do you have a copy of the deed that has been recorded with the county for my review?

- Do you have a clear title on the property as far as you know?

- Do you have a general warranty deed on the property?

- How soon can you produce a clear title policy?

- If I can pay all your closing cost will you consider a lower sales price?

- Is this property cross collateralized with another property you own?

- If so, which type of property?

- What is the address of the other property?

NOTE: If seller has a special warranty deed, quit-clams deed or anything other than a general warranty deed seek more research or ask if he has any addition paper work?

- Which title company was used in the previous closing of the property?

- Ask the seller if they have any of the previous closing paperwork such as :

  - Title commitment

  - Deed

  - Escrow Agent

  - Name of Attorney

  - Settlement statement or Closing statement

4) FINDING OUT ABOUT LIENS, PROPERTY TAXES, AND LAWSUITS

- Do you have the tax id number or parcel number for the property?

- What were last year's property taxes?

- Do you have any tax suits on the property?

- Are the current year of property taxes paid?

- Are there any back taxes that are owed on the property?

- If yes, how many years of property taxes are delinquent?

- Ask them, if they have the total amount of delinquent property taxes that are due?

- Do they have a payment plan set up with the county?

- Do they have any receipts of any payments towards the property taxes?

- Are you currently in any type of lawsuit with this property?

- Has this property ever been in any type of lawsuit?

- If so, what was the outcome of that lawsuit?

- If a judgment is the response, what kind of judgment does the property have?

- Are there any liens, judgments, or mortgages on the property that you are aware of?

- If yes, what type of liens, specifically?

- How did you get a lien on your property?

- How much is the lien or liens?

- Do you owe a mortgage on your property?

- If so, what kind of mortgage do you have?

- How much do you still owe on the mortgage?

- What is the interest rate? And is it a fixed or variable interest rate?

- If a variable interest rate, ask what the life cap rate is and ask how much can the interest rate change per year?

- How many years are left on the mortgage?

- Any pre-payment penalties?

- Have you refinanced the property since the original purchase?

- If so, how much did you refinance for?

- When was the refinance?

- What percentage of leverage do you have on the property? (50%, 60%, etc.)

- Which lender did you use?

- Would you recommend that lender to me?

5) GETTING TENANT AND MANAGEMENT INFORMATION ABOUT THE DWELLING

- Who manages the property?

- If owner says themselves, Ask them is they have any experience running multi-family dwellings?

- If they do have experience, how much and what kind of experience?

- Is there an on-site manager?

- If no, why not?

- If there is an on-site manager, how much do they get paid and do they get free rent?

- Is there an on-site maintenance man?

- If no, why not?

- If there is an on-site maintenance man, how much does he get paid and does he get free rent?

- Is there a management company that runs the dwelling?

- Is there a current rent roll I can see?

- Do the tenants have copies of their leases?

- How do you except rents? Mail or drop-slot? (cash, money order, direct deposit, or checks)

- How many delinquent payers do you current have?

- How often arc they delinquent?

- Is the dwelling an all bills paid dwelling where the utilities are paid by the owner?

- Is so, what bills or utilities are paid?

- What kind of cooling system is there for the dwelling? (Individual A/C condenser units, individual window units, chiller systems, etc.)

- What kind of heating system is there for the dwelling?

- What year was the dwelling built?

- Have there been any updates or remodeling done since the dwelling was built?

- If so, what were they and who did the work?

6) <u>DURING THE TOUR OF THE DWELLING</u>

- Ask to see the boiler room?

- **<u>NOTE</u>**: Check the boiler room for broken or repaired water pipes.

- How old is the boiler (hot water heater) or boilers?

- Has it ever been repaired or replaced since you (the seller) have owned the dwelling?

- If so, what kind of repair was done and how much was that repair?

- If replaced, Ask how much it cost and to see a receipt if able?

- Ask to see a ready to move in to unit?

- **<u>NOTE</u>**: Check the craftsmanship of the work done to each unit. Look for: overspray paint, kitchen and bathroom counters, mirrors, etc.

- Ask to see every unit of the complex

- Then ask to see the worst if not all the down units? (needs repairs)

CHAPTER 6

<u>QUESTIONS FOR THE SELLERS TO THE BUYERS</u>

1) SCREENING A POTENTIAL BUYER FOR A SINGLE-FAMILY HOME

- Have the potential buyer fill out an applicant

- Get a Driver license or ID, Social Security Card, and make sure they match.

- Make copies of ID's if necessary.

- Complete a back ground check thru DPS, sex offenders list, and thru your online 3rd party search.

- If anything comes up, you as the seller make up what you are willing to deal with.

- It's good to check for evictions, broken leases, foreclosures, and so on.

- Do a credit check if financing takes place. You want to make sure the potential buyer can pay and you do not have to struggle to get your money.

- How soon are you looking to buy a house?

- You may not have all your living arrangements met at the next location you are moving to.

- You might even need time to move or pack?

- What do you like about that area of town?

- Will you compensate me if I find you the right house?

- What price range were you interested in?

- Is there a house in the area you are interested in that you have had your eye on?

- If so how can I help?

- Can you tell me more about that house?

- Do you need help negotiating the contract?

- What is your schedule like to look at properties?

- Are you considering financing the property?

- Are you pre-qualified?

- What is your source of income?

- Do you except any large amounts of money any time soon?

- Do you have money to repair to remodel the house?

- Are you willing to look at fixer-uppers?

- Are you interested in seller finance properties?

- What can you afford to pay per month?

- What part of town are you looking to buy in?

- What 3rd party references do you have for the seller to consider seller finance?

- Have you ever been evicted from a property?

- Have you ever had a broken lease?

- Have you ever been a foreclosure?

- Have you ever owned a home before?

- Do you have any land lord references I can call?

2) SCREENING A POTENTIAL BUYER FOR RAW LAND OR VACANT LOT

- Have the potential buyer fill out an applicant

- Get a Driver license or ID, Social Security Card, and make sure they match.

- Make copies of ID's if necessary.

- Complete a back ground check thru DPS, sex offenders list, and thru your online 3rd party search.

- If anything comes up, you as the seller make up what you are willing to deal with.

- It's good to check for evictions, broken leases, foreclosures, and so on.

- Do a credit check if financing takes place. You want to make sure the potential buyer can pay and you do not have to struggle to get your money.

- How soon are you looking to buy some land?

- Are you looking for wooded property or already cleared land?

- What are your plans for the property?

- Are you going to live there or build investments?

- Have you seen any other properties in the area?

- What do you like about this area of town?

- Will you compensate me if I find you the right land you want?

- What price range were you interested in?

- How much are you looking to finance?

- What sort of down payment do you have?

- Is there a land in the area you are interested in that you have had your eye on?

- If so how can I help?

- Can you tell me more about that land you seen in the area?

- Do you need help negotiating the contract?

- What is your schedule like to look at properties?

- Are you considering financing the property?

- Are you pre-qualified?

- What is your source of income?

- Do you except any large amounts of money any time soon?

- Do you have money to repair to remodel the house?

- Are you willing to look at fixer-uppers?

- Are you interested in seller finance properties?

- What can you afford to pay per month?

- What part of town are you looking to buy in?

- What 3rd party references do you have for the seller to consider seller finance?

- Have you ever been a foreclosure?

- Do you know what permits you will need to complete your project?

- Do you have a licensed contractor for the project?

- Do you have your engineers for the project?

-

3) SCREENING A POTENTIAL BUYER FOR A MULTI-FAMILY DWELLING

- Have the potential buyer fill out an applicant

- Get a Driver license or ID, Social Security Card, and make sure they match.

- Make copies of ID's if necessary.

- Complete a back ground check thru DPS, sex offenders list, and thru your online 3rd party search.

- If anything comes up, you as the seller make up what you are willing to deal with.

- It's good to check for evictions, broken leases, foreclosures, and so on.

- Do a credit check if financing takes place. You want to make sure the potential buyer can pay and you do not have to struggle to get your money.

- Do you have any experience in purchasing multi-family building?

- Have you ever own a multi-family dwelling?

- What do you need to make a decision?

- How soon are you looking to buy a multi-family dwelling?

- Have you looked into owner occupied dwellings?

- What do you like about that area of town?

- Will you compensate me if I find you the right property?

- What price range were you interested in?

- How many units are you looking to manage?

- Is there a certain area you are interested in purchasing a multi-family dwelling?

- If so how can I help?

- Can you tell me more about the criteria you have in mind?

- Do you need help negotiating the sells contract?

- What is your schedule like to look at properties?

- Are you considering financing the property?

- Are you pre-qualified?

- What is your source of income?

- Do you except any large amounts of money any time soon?

- Do you have money to repair to remodel the multi-family dwelling?

- Do you have money to manage the property?

- Do you know how will manage the property?

- Are you willing to look at fixer-uppers?

- Are you interested in seller finance properties?

- What 3rd party references do you have for the seller to consider seller finance?

- Do you currently own any real estate properties?

- If so, what kind?

And the list continues with you and your inputs please send me an email with any suggestions.

CHAPTER 7

<u>FINAL THOUGHTS</u>

I would like to end this book with a few key tips and some great motivational quotes as well as some must read books.

Remember what you have learned in this book and refer to this book as many times as possibly. Let's recap on what we've went over in this book. You learned what it takes to build your career or interest in real estate. You learned about understanding terminology, eliminating time wasters and non-winners from your potentially buy list. But the most important thing you learned is about doing your own due diligence. Remember to always do your own research! If you do not know how please go to the internet and search how to do your own research. That might be my next book, send your comments to my email in my Contact Info page on page number # 99

In closing, I hope that these lists will help you become more aware and become more prepared at acquiring real estate. Together we have completed the book; the only thing left to do is implement the book. If you find this book useful please send me a comment or letter explaining how this book helped you or someone you know. All my contact information is on the last page of this book; feel free to make any suggestions, questions, or concerns.

MOTIVATIONAL QUOTES

"Never mistake activity for achievement" – John Wooden

"I am always doing things I cannot do, that's how I get to do them" – Pablo Picasso

"Take the fast nickel over the slow dime" – Roy Powers

"Real estate is easy, people are difficult" – Del Wamlesy

"The first and the best victory is to conquer self" – Plato

"The shortest way to do many things is to do only one thing at a time" – Mozart

"You must have long term goals to keep you from being frustrated by short term failures"- Charles C. Noble

"What you get by achieving your goals is not as important as what you become by achieving your goals" - Zig Ziglar

"If the clothes make the man; then the exterior of the building makes the business" –Unknown

MUST READ BOOKS

Richest Man in Babylon
Author: George S. Clason

How to make Friends and Influence People-
Author: Dale Carnegie

The Quick & Easy Way To Effective Speaking
Author: Dale Carnegie

The Millionaire Mind
Author: Thomas J Stanley, Ph.D.

Think and Grow Rich
Author: Napoleon Hill

Confessions of a Real Estate Entrepreneur
Author: James A. Randel

The Road to Riches:
Author: Napoleon Hill

Time Management:
Author: Brian Tracy

How to Win in Commercial Real Estate Investing
Author: Craig R. Coppola, CRE, SIOR, CCIM

Creating Your Own Real Estate Cash Machine
Author: Alan Schnur

First, Break All The Rules
Author: Marcus Buckingham & Curt Coffman

The Way To Wealth
Author: Benjamin Franklin

Zero To One
Author: Peter Thiel with Blake Masters

The Smartest Guys In The Room
Author:

Thinking Fast and Slow
Author: Daniel Kahneman

The Contrarian Playbook
Author: Manny Khoshbin

The Autobiography of Benjamin Franklin
Author:

The Gospel of Wealth
Author: Andrew Carnegie

The Problem is the Solution
Author: Judy Cook

Contact Info

Email: <u>UpoaHouston@yahoo.com</u>

Mailing Address:
P.o. Box 1280
Manvel, TX 77578

www.ingramcontent.com/pod-product-compliance
Lightning Source LLC
Chambersburg PA
CBHW030906180526
45163CB00004B/1728